DESTINATION VS DESTINATION

NEENA PRABHAKAR

BLUEROSE PUBLISHERS
India | U.K.

Copyright © Neena Prabhakhar 2024

All rights reserved by author. No part of this publication may be reproduced, stored in a retrieval system or transmitted in any form or by any means, electronic, mechanical, photocopying, recording or otherwise, without the prior permission of the author. Although every precaution has been taken to verify the accuracy of the information contained herein, the publisher assumes no responsibility for any errors or omissions. No liability is assumed for damages that may result from the use of information contained within.

BlueRose Publishers takes no responsibility for any damages, losses, or liabilities that may arise from the use or misuse of the information, products, or services provided in this publication.

For permissions requests or inquiries regarding this publication, please contact:

BLUEROSE PUBLISHERS
www.BlueRoseONE.com
info@bluerosepublishers.com
+91 8882 898 898
+4407342408967

ISBN: 978-93-5741-453-1

Cover Design: Muskan Sachdeva
Typesetting: Pooja Sharma

First Edition: March 2024

In your presence, there's fullness of joy

In your aura, there's divinity and mysticism

Rajeev Verma

Shri Shri Hari

About the Author

As a 57-year-old mother of two, Neena has experienced many of life's challenges and joys. But it wasn't until she underwent a spiritual transformation that she truly discovered her calling as a writer.

Through her new perspective on life, Neena has found a renewed sense of purpose and creativity. Her writing is deeply introspective, exploring themes of love, loss, redemption, and the power of the human spirit to overcome adversity. She draws on her own life experiences, as well as her spiritual insights, to create compelling stories and essays that resonate with readers on a profound level.

As a writer, Neena is committed to sharing her message of spiritual transformation and personal growth with others. She believes that everyone has the power to transform their lives and find meaning and purpose in their own unique way. Through her writing, she hopes to inspire and uplift others and help them discover their own inner wisdom and strength.

Contents

My Life 1

God's Realisation 35

The Guru 38

The World of Higher Consciousness 55

Naad 61

Mysticism of Guruji 63

Turn of Events 65

The Silence 69

My Life

Dear reader, I have been born twice. Once, when I was taken out of my mother's womb, and then, when I met Guruji, I was born again. So, naturally, it would have been much better if I started off with my journey into the mystic pathways of spirituality, but then again, without knowing what came before it, you would be left clueless.

And my purpose here is to not make you more confused, but to have you settle in to get a glimpse of my carnation and incarnation in the same lifetime. And if you are able to get anything out of my ups to face your downs, then, dear reader, that would be our victory. As we are both going to walk the same path now. It would be better if we got acquainted.

As for me, I was the eldest of four siblings. My mother was a teacher in a government school in Punjab, and my father had left his job to build his own business. I never knew him personally, so all I know about him is from others, and what I have gathered is that he was not very stable in his earnings. And as a result of this, at the tender age of five months, I was sent to my maternal grandmother's place in Delhi. From then on, that place was my home.

Dear reader, have you ever looked back at your life and found points where, had the circumstances been a little more favourable for you, your lives would have been different? I have many, and this is probably the first in a series of them. My grandmother's family included my grandmother, my grandfather, an aunt (my uncle's wife) and one unmarried maternal aunt. Since I had no other option, I made them my family too. I mean, I know they were already my family, but having people in your family and making them your family are two different things, aren't they? Back then, I wasn't much of a diary person, so I do not have much to look back on. I only have vague memories of how my life was back then, but I do remember that I was brought up by my mother. My maternal aunt. And she was, in fact, literally maa si (like mother) for me, for I used to consider her my mother until I was made aware. But we can only have good things for as long as we can, because soon she got married and moved on with her own life. It was around the same time that my younger sister was also put in my Nani's care.

Initially, I did not like that even a little bit. But this feeling didn't last long, as slowly and gradually I developed a beautiful bond with her, and before I knew it, we were partners in our happiness and sorrows.

Don't get me wrong. My Nani's place was comfortable. But even with all the riches around, the ache and the urge to know your real family were always there. You can only try to fill in the hole in your heart to know that what you have been missing all your life is just a family to acknowledge and love you. For me, this was a distant dream. Usually, the ache was just a noise in the background, but when our classmates in school talked about their parents, we couldn't help but sit quietly and listen to the life we could not have.

As I said, I have no complaints about how our lives were at my Nani's place. My maternal grandparents were usually very considerate of us. Until their sons and daughters, my maternal uncles and aunts, would come to India for a vacation from abroad, then they used to become indifferent towards our existence. And this went on for three or four months, every year. Some of them didn't mind staying, and some were sympathetic. Yet, there were a few who were outright rude and understood the whole scenario as our father's inability to take care of us.

Otherwise, why would someone throw their kids at the mercy of their maternal grandparents? Some of these aunts would abuse us and treat us as servants, and no one would listen to our sufferings. Not even our mother, who would also act indifferent in such matters.

During this period of my life, all I had was my sister, and all she had was me. We did what we could to help each other strive. We gave each other the strength to live a day at a time, waiting for their visit to be over. Because once they went back, things would turn back to normal. Even though we could never get the normal we wanted, we still find that normal preferable given our circumstances. We got used to this pattern, and this continued until my entire childhood. It was in this environment that I completed my schooling and then got my graduation. While these small incidents kept repeating and leaving deep marks on our inner selves,

As I grew older and experienced more of what life had to offer, I came to understand this simple fact: no matter what type of comfort we are brought up with, if we don't have someone to listen to us, understand us, and guide us, it means nothing. Because this is when our lives and we ourselves are taking shape. We are just beginning to understand the wonder that is the world and are getting ready to face it and walk our own paths. And if one is left alone at this time, then, more often than not, they tend to have this hollowness throughout their lives. They also tend to develop into people according to their own whims. As was I.

I grew up into a young, beautiful, and strong-headed woman, despite these challenges. As there were no strong male figures in my life, I was quite independent from the very start. In these matters, I was heavily influenced by my grandmother, who was of a very strong character. In her own way, she drilled down her good values in me, made me down to earth, respected my elders, and taught me not to hold grudges against anyone. Values that I still carry with me today and try to pass on to my children.

My maternal aunt got married when I was five years old. She used to visit us frequently, and as I have already told you, I shared this beautiful bond with her. Something that I did not share with my own mother, even though she used to visit us three or four times a year and take care of our financial needs. But there was always something missing. Neither she made any efforts to be the mother I needed, nor did I try to make things better. Slowly, I had stopped caring. Or maybe, at that age, I didn't care about such things that much at all. These were the things I started understanding when I became a mother myself and tried to give my children what I never could.

But it was not all bad, dear reader. Every life is a treasure trove of good and bad memories.

And when I look back, I find a fair share of both to look back on. Let me tell you about something that I really cherish festivals! I know it might not seem like a big deal today, but when it's all.

become a competition about spending money and what not. But back then, it was a huge thing. We used to celebrate them together and enjoy them.

I can still feel that old, festive spirit in the air. I can still almost touch it. Whether it be Diwali, Dussehra, Holi, or some other small festival, each one of them meant something, and my grandmother celebrated all of them with great vigour. We used to go and see Ramleela for ten consecutive days. And I personally used to feel very heartbroken on the tenth, as I never wanted them to end. Me and my sister would become infatuated with the person who would be playing the role of Lord Rama, and after the festival, we would try to find out his address and stalk him. Not creepily, of course! And yes, this is one of those small memories that I look back on with some fondness.

Youth is the time to dream, and like every nineteen-year-old woman of my age, I also dreamt of having a perfect guy in my life who would love me and cherish me. And with these fantasies in my head, I fell in love with a guy who lived in our locality. I did not exactly know where he lived, but the moment I saw him for the first time in the market, I was in love. I can still remember it as if it were yesterday. You rarely forget your first love, and you rarely can put how you exactly felt in words. I can still remember that when I looked at him, the universe came to a standstill, and only we were there looking into each other's eyes. Even though it was for a moment, I felt like an eternity had passed. For some time, I was swinging in the skies, and the world suddenly seemed so beautiful. I was not myself anymore.

We started seeing each other, but like everything good in life, it came to an end after a year when his family pressured him to not see a girl from outside their caste.

Meanwhile, things were not that good in my own house. My other two siblings were living with my parents, and because of the daily fights, my brother dropped out and got into drugs. This made situations really tense, as he would demand money and, at times, even come to my grandmother's house and steal or snatch things from us. We were already looked down upon by our relatives, and this just added to it. This resulted in several fights at home, where we would be very hostile towards him, and we even sent him to several rehab centers, but every time we sent him, he would come out the same.

This was around the time when I started feeling pain in every joint of my body. I went and saw several doctors, but none of them were able to diagnose what the problem was with me until we were suggested to see this one doctor. He got some blood tests done, and it turned out that I was RApositive, and arthritis has spread severely through my entire body. I was having difficulties doing even the most basic daily chores. I started taking high-dose painkillers, which in turn caused several other complications in my body. Amidst my dropping health, the family discord, and my breakup, I felt vulnerable and started looking for solace outside my family again.

There was no one to really touch or reach my heart. Even though my grandmother took good care of me, she would take me to the doctor and give me all the proper medical attention she could. But I used to feel as if something was missing. I would cry through the nights, and nothing would change. Soon, my growing age became a concern for the family, and talks about my marriage started making the rounds. All my relatives started pointing this out to my mother, who, under this pressure, started requesting that they search for prospective grooms. But none of them would do anything, and her pleas would go to deaf ears. I still don't understand how just marrying someone would make someone's life better. But still, I took the task into my own hands and thought, if not anyone else, I would search for a groom myself.

Later, when I became a mother myself and saw my life from a different angle, I came to deeply understand that what one gives to one's children matters a lot in the long run. I am not talking about material things, but things like anxiety, fear, insecurity, and pessimism, which we knowingly or unknowingly pass onto our children. These things have a long-lasting impact on the children's growth.

A child is a blank slate in the beginning. If one writes the wrong things, then these wrong things will get imprinted forever on those young minds. So, when parents are bringing up their children, it is very important how they are bringing them up. Some parents tend to think that kids can be raised on their own, but what I feel and understand is that they need to be observed, tended to, and taken good care of. Only then will one be able to raise them as capable individuals.

Growing up, I did not have these privileges. I grew up with my insecurities and my fickle mind. When I planned to find a life partner for myself, around that time, a family moved into our neighborhood. It seemed to be a nice family with an older married man with his two kids, an older lady, and a young man. I had already finished my graduation by then. And after a one-year break, I started my post-graduation. I was very good at studying. I did not have to put much effort into getting good marks in the examinations.

I observed our neighbors for some time and then decided that the young son would be the right guy for me. He had a good business, a nice house, and a car of his own. He was already of marriageable age and showed interest in me. So, after a year of their shifting, we started dating. We would meet for some time and talk. Things were okay for once. It seemed like this was it, and we could go ahead with marriage. We talked with our families, and everyone seemed to agree except my father, whom I have rarely met. He was not okay with this alliance and outright refused, making it clear that if I went ahead with it, he wouldn't come to my marriage. He was not going to let me marry the man I chose, nor was he ready to look for a suitable match for me. Things got complicated. My health started to deteriorate day by day.

I used to take medicine in those days, which had either cin or sin in the end, and I used to ponder what sin I had done to go through this much pain. I endured, and so did the questions. The pressure to marry increased as my younger sister was also reaching a marriageable age. Since my dad didn't like the boy, I found for myself, I asked my mother to search for a match for my sister, and I decided to go ahead with the MPhil I had gotten admission to. I wanted to carry on with my academics, get a PhD, and then become a lecturer. But she did not agree. It was important for the older sister to get married first for society. My education was made secondary. For her, that could be done even after my marriage. It was as if she also believed in marriage being the only solution to every problem. Maybe it was for her, but not for me. She could have very well gone ahead with the marriage of my younger sister and left me out of this mess, but I was to live a different life.

I got engaged as I was finishing my post-graduation. Just a few days before our marriage, my fiancé revealed his biggest secret. That shook my life. The family he was living with was not his family; rather, his real family lived in another part of the city. Even his business was not his. I was taken aback. I did not know what to do. It was too late to step back. With a heavy heart, I went ahead.

I have the belief that I will make this marriage work and will support and encourage my husband-to-be to work hard. His family had eight siblings and a widowed mother. The conditions were not that good. It was only later that I realised how many secrets were kept from us. How many lies were told regarding his qualifications and his life? He was not even a graduate. He was much older than what they told me. Anyone hearing this would call me a fool to go ahead with this, but I did not want to be the reason for another trouble in the family. I was confident that I would get out of this difficult situation and things would turn out well in the end, but destiny had different ideas. Just after I completed my post-graduation, I got married.

See, my mother was very happy as her biggest responsibility was taken care of. She could not have been happier. But all the merriment was not long-lived. Just before we were to tie our destinies together, he showed us his cards. Everything we had known about him until then was all a lie. He had no business, no house, and no cars of his own. Everything was owned by his cousins. In fact, the family he was living with was not his. He had a job in a factory. This looks like a scene straight out of a movie. Everything came crashing down. But, till then, I was too deep in it to back down. Not with all the things that were at stake. Our society, in certain ways, can be unforgiving, and with all that I was going through, I did not want to go there. So, I agreed. Still. Going against all my senses and conscience, I went ahead with the arrangement. I did not know any better. I had no belief in myself, and I knew the situation my family was in. Adding to this, my health was falling, so I did not feel like I had any choice. I got married.

My life changed that day. My in-laws had a decent place. I took a sigh of relief. But that was all the relief I was going to get, because on the first night of our marriage, my husband got terribly drunk. He started abusing me and then tried to commit suicide by hanging himself with the cloth my mother used to tie our fates together. I was just twenty-two. I never knew many men in my life. My and my father were a mystery to me. This was my first step in man's world, and it was traumatic.

After that, my life became a living hell. I mean, looking at how it started, I could not even say that I was surprised. He would drink every day. Without even bothering whether there was food in the house or not. And it was not just him. They were eight siblings, and all his brothers were heavy drinkers. They did not care much about the financial situation and spent most of what they earned on drinking. I was broken, and I was broken. I did not know what to do. My health was deteriorating rapidly. My doctor told me that I would end up in a wheelchair soon, as my arthritis was getting worse day by day. All the doors seemed to be closed. And in these conditions, I became the mother of two boys.

Raising two kids in such a situation might sound impossible. But somehow, I managed. Shuffling between my grandmother's house and my in-laws, I took on all the responsibilities of my boys. I was not going to leave them with anyone. They were not going to get the life I lived. I was resolved. No matter what it takes, I was ready to give everything I had to make sure that they got a life worth living.

I took up a job when my younger son was two and a half and ready to go to school. My employment changed things for the better. But still, not everything was good in my family. My relations with my in-laws were good, but I could not say the same for my husband. He became more abusive. He would beat me every now and then. I continued staying with him because I saw no other option. They were different days. But I did not let that affect my kids. I had a job that paid enough to give them an education and put food on the table.

But I did not have a suitable qualification. It was not like I was bad at studying. Quite the opposite. I was the top student in my Masters, and I even got direct admission to MPhil because of that. I always wanted to pursue a PhD from Delhi University. I wanted to study more. But it was all in the past. My mother was not ready to let me study and marry my younger sister, even though I requested it, because of society. For her, the elder daughter had to be married first. I tried to reason. I even found a guy and asked her to get me engaged and then look for suitable matches for my younger sister. But it did not work out. I had to relent.

By this time, my sister had introduced me to Buddhism, and I had become a devout practitioner. I found hope in my religion. Somehow, I got some relief from my arthritis, and my limbs started working normally. I was twenty-seven. I did not have any suitable qualifications for a job. Therefore, I spent six months doing a computer course, which led to my getting employed. The pay was not that good. I could provide for my children for some time, but I could see that it would not be enough once they went to higher classes. I needed to earn money. Automatically, I turned to business.

I had started working in the marketing division of an advertising agency. I had always been good with people—talking to them, forming relationships, and just knowing them. It was a small agency, but I was doing a good job. We were a team of five: a designer, a photographer, two other staff, and I was the marketing head. After a few years, the three of us thought of starting our own agency. We quit our jobs and formed our own company.

My colleagues would come to my house to discuss things related to the business. My husband would be on his best behaviour, even in front of them. He would abuse me in front of them, and sometimes he would even raise his hand. I felt pathetic. Seeing how things were going, one of my partners offered to take care of me and asked me to leave my husband. That was shocking! I was the mother of two, and he was seven years younger. Initially, even he insisted that I leave the kids and move in with him, but I was clear from day one. My kids came with me. I brought them into this world, and I had it on my own shoulders to give them a good life. Seeing my determination, he agreed to take care of them as well.

After eleven years of my first marriage, at the age of thirty-two, I left my husband and got married to him. It was not an easy thing to do in a country like India. It still is not. I became a topic of discussion among my relatives and neighbors. Sometimes it would get to me. I will feel disturbed. But then I would see my kids, and I would put on a brave face. Just for their sake. Even he did not ever insist on meeting his children. Without taking a single penny from him or the dowry that he got at my wedding, I left his house with just my kids and the clothes we were wearing.

I had no financial or social support. My mother and my sisters had also refused to lend me a helping hand, as they felt that doing so would affect their social status. Our business was new, so we were not making much money. I had to leave Delhi and get my sons out of their schools as I could not handle the expenses. We moved to a semi-furnished flat in Karnal. I would travel from Karnal to Delhi three times a week because of my business. I did this for around six months. It is common sense that any business relies on marketing. With so much on my plate, I was not able to put all my focus into it. So, after a lot of contemplation, I decided to put my kids in the hostel of their school and move back to Delhi again.

They studied at Tagore Bal Niketan. The school, which Kalpana Chawla also attended, had its own hostel, but again, money was a problem. I asked for help from a cousin of mine who lived in England. The decision was heartbreaking for me. I had never thought that I would ever leave them. But I consoled myself. I was doing this for them only. With a heavy heart, I came back to Delhi.

After the deaths of my grandparents, my uncle made it clear that I was not to set foot in that house. I had nowhere to go. So, I started spending my nights sleeping on the floor in the office. In the morning, I would use the same place to talk to my clients. I started my business with a broken chair, table, and computer, which I bought in installments. All from scratch. I devoted myself to it as if my life depended on it. Because for me, that business held the keys to a bright future for my kids.

But again, I am too trusting. I put everything in my new husband's name. I felt obliged that I owed him that for taking me and my children out of that hellhole. An aunt of mine had a two-bedroom flat in a very remote area in Rohini with no connectivity. I gathered some courage and asked her to lend me the flat, as she was living in England. She handed me the keys, and I, along with my husband, started living there. Our business started growing, and at one point I even started musing about bringing my kids back. I knew I could not afford expensive private schools, but still, I got them admitted to a decent school for the upcoming new session. Just the thought of having them back to live with me made me blissful.

For a moment, everything was going fine. My husband loved me. Things were okay. I became a bridge between my kids and their stepfather to help them adjust. And they started adjusting. They grew so attached to each other that sometimes I started feeling like the odd one out. But that was okay for me. All I ever wanted was a happy place to call home, and I finally had one.

We had started an export business, and our efforts were finally bearing fruit. We now had money to afford some luxuries. We got a car and purchased a better office space, which we renovated and decorated aesthetically. Three days a week, I would go to my office and work, and the rest of the days I would be at home. It became a routine. Together, we marketed rigorously. At places where I could not go alone, I had my husband accompany me. Nothing came between us and our business. We were out there in extreme summer, winter, and rain. Soon, our business spread throughout the northern part of the country.

I did not yet put my boys in a better school, as I was saving money for their higher education. There were some issues in the family, but they were easily manageable. To support and help my children in their studies, I thought of taking a break from the office. My husband was okay with it. So, I started staying back. He did not like me practicing Buddhism, so I had stopped that as well. I was ready to do anything to make this marriage work. I started doing all the household chores and focused on my kids. Initially, I had difficulties settling in because this was never the life I wanted to live. But slowly, I got used to it.

After a few months, I started noticing a change in the behaviour of my husband. He had slowly started to withdraw the financial support and became distant. Initially, it did not bother me. But then, I had had my share of lessons from life. It was very disturbing for me. He stopped giving me any money and started running the house on his own. I wouldn't have a penny in my wallet and was again surviving on the bare minimums. This got to me. I decided to join my business again. But then I was bluntly told to never set foot in the office. It does not belong to you anymore, he said. I was shocked. It was all the same again.

We started fighting at home. I started having my suspicions. One day I saw some messages on his phone, which gave substance to my anxious thoughts. He was having an affair with a much younger girl in our office. I started sinking into depression once again. We stopped talking, and just for the sake of my growing kids, I continued to act normal. But his behaviour degraded as the days passed. He became less interested in my life and my condition. He started a comfortable life of his own. It went on for three years, while I languished penniless, hopeless, depressed, and miserable.

It is truly said that the more you suppress something, the harder it will bounce back. And my thoughts, emotions, feelings, and thoughts were on overdrive. I knew what a broken family did to children, so I was still trying to compromise. Anything to make sure that they had a family as they grew up, and grow up, they did. In no time, it was time for their higher education, and my husband refused to offer any help. According to him, the business was not doing well, and therefore, he had no money to fund my children's education. This was a big blow to me. Because despite whatever was happening, I felt like he wouldn't be able to rob me of this. I made that business to help my kids, and now... All of this was getting too much for me, and under this pressure, one day I decided to end it all. But my older son, who was in 12th grade at the time, saved me.

He encouraged me to take charge of my life all over again. I had once done it, and he said he believed that I could do it again. I can once again make a difference in my life and theirs. This was in 2007. It was New Year's Day, and I was in bed until 2 in the afternoon. I took the words of my son to heart and decided enough was enough. I started practicing Buddhism again. I started to accept things that happened in my life and tried to move on. Slowly and gradually, I felt myself coming out of the pits of depression. But again, I did not know of any miracle to arrange for my son's higher education in this short amount of time.

My cousin, who lived in England, had promised me that she would support my kids' education. I had tried too hard to do everything on my own, but seeing that I had no other choice left, I called in her favor. She willingly supported the higher education of both my sons. Meanwhile, after 7 years of being at home, I once again got a job at the age of 42. This time I started working at a school. Being financially independent again brought a little happiness back into my life. I felt complete again.

My biggest worries were solved. I was no longer at the mercy of my 'husband', and my boys were also pursuing their studies. All my husband contributed to the so-called family was 1/4th of the total household expenses, what he believed to be his share in the family. I did not say anything, as all I wanted was just peace.

My elder son completed his BTech and got a job at a software company in Bangalore. The younger one first did a BBA and then an MBA. When he was in his last semester, my husband declared that he was moving out because he had to look after his mother, who lived in the village. He said the business was done for, and so he would be looking for other opportunities along with his brother. The news still shocked me, as I had been hopeful all this time. I had been waiting for things to get better, and I believed that maybe they would. I requested that he stay, but his mind was made up. Despite my requests, in November 2016, he moved out.

If this had happened earlier, I would have moved past it. I mean, when you have young kids to take care of, you don't realise how fast time flies. But now my sons were all grown up and had flown out. I was left alone. Although my job kept me busy, I was shattered. The silence in my house killed me. I could not sleep. My blood pressure shot up. I got diagnosed with trigeminal neuralgia, an incurable disease, and sank into depression once again. Since my childhood, I have kept yearning for a family. I endured it all with a smiling face to keep my broken family after broken family together, but I failed every time. At the end of the day, I was back to where I started. Even though this time it was a little different, My sons took very good care of me, and they were deeply concerned about my situation. But what could they have done? I was slowly losing all hope in myself and just started dragging my body to fulfil my responsibilities.

My husband stopped showing any concern for me. He would call twice a day and visit for one night a month, but all his attention was on the well-being of the kids. His reasoning was that people continue to live even after the death of their loved ones, so I should assume that he is no more and carry on. I wish it were that easy!

We knew each other for twenty years, and it was not easy at all for me to let go. He would come and go, and after he was gone, I would cry for days. Nothing was going right in my world. My health was getting worse again. It was getting difficult for me to face the outer world. All I wanted to do was just close myself up in a room and never come out of it. I decided to leave my job. But the vice principal refused to accept my resignation and asked me to go on leave for a few days and sort myself out.

Gradually, I started to come to terms with my situation. It was not easy, but it was not impossible anymore. It wasn't like he stopped coming. He still did. But now his presence and his absence meant the same to me. I started writing a blog, and writing helped my mind to be at peace. I felt successful, and I was happy. To keep myself busier, I started a business, which really helped me open again. I started travelling abroad for my business things were coming back to normal once again. Since we were not getting anywhere in this relationship, I asked my husband to stop calling me and stop visiting me. My elder son was in touch with him, and he felt that I was not doing the right thing by stopping all my relations with him. But I wanted to move on. I wanted to live my life.

I started getting busy in my daily life. I went to school, handled my business, and wrote my blog. These were the joys of my life. In the meantime, my elder son applied for his PR in Australia and moved there within six months. My younger son was also getting regular promotions. After 7 years, things were getting back to normal. When my older son was in Bangalore, he came into a relationship with a girl who was a fashion designer. They decided to get married, and I gave them my blessings. But my elder son put in a condition that he wanted his stepfather to be a part of the celebration and asked for my permission to come. Reluctantly, I agreed. Even though he had no significant role to play. He would just come and go, pretending to know everything about the ongoing preparations, and would leave after a day.

I left my job to focus on the wedding preparations. My business has also started doing well, so I felt that I could take the risk. But still, watching my son marry was making me think about things that I always just wished for but never had. Watching the kid I raised with a partner made me feel the absence of one in my own life. I also wanted to have someone to talk to, discuss my ideas with, and share things over a cup of tea. I wanted someone to sit with. This resulted in a small fling who died the same death as my preceding relationships.

It was all devastating for me. I started feeling somehow responsible for all of this. All of this was my fault. I started questioning why I am unable to carry on relationships with men in my life. Why do I keep going through the same cycle again and again? These questions started to haunt me and made me more and more depressed.

One day, I was feeling low. Nothing was working to lift me up. So, I decided to visit my cousin at the Safdarjung Development Area. We decided that we would meet in the afternoon at 12. I got up late and was able to reach there only by 3:30. Even talking with her was not making any difference. I was as restless as I ever could be. Suddenly, a business associate of mine saw me there and offered to drop me off at Cannaught Place, as I had some work there and had planned to go after meeting my sister. I decided to leave early. He requested that he make a quick stop on the way for some urgent work, and at that time, I was not in the mood to do anything else. So I just tagged along.

I did not know what fate had in reserve for me. On the way, he stopped at a Shiva temple. I went inside the temple with him. The temple had been there for the last seventy years. An old building built in a very nice and serene place in one of the poshest areas of Delhi. The priest explained that the linga in the temple emerged while a person was digging the earth to build his house. That very night, Lord Shiva came in his dreams and told him to enshrine it at this specific place. The story intrigued me. I started feeling the peace that people associate with places of worship.

After completing my puja, I stood outside for some time. Suddenly, I felt a gentle and divine-looking figure emerge from my right side. For a moment, I just kept staring. I was drawn to him, and my inner conscience and my inner voice encouraged me to go talk to him. The figure was moving towards his car, so I rushed to him. I asked if he was some kind of priest who dabbled in astrology or palmistry. He laughed and denied it. He said he can only tell me about himself by just looking at me. This got me and my friend interested. We asked him about ourselves.

Slowly, we became engrossed in his speech. He kept talking, and the time flew by, and we did not even realise it. Just his presence alone was calming my restlessness, and I was able to relate to what he was saying. We stood by his side for around two hours, and we were so excited that we had goosebumps even after he left. The meeting was sudden, but so fulfilling and enriching. I thought of putting his suggestions and advice into practice.

When I asked him about myself, the first thing he said was that despite achieving so many things and achieving so much, even after overcoming so much, I never appreciated myself. It rang true. It was strong; yes, I had very low self-esteem. I had always been like this. The second thing he told me was that I am a great manifester, so no matter how impossible things appear, I will always be able to achieve anything that I desire. Now, I can see the truth in his words. I was unable to see it before because I was too busy doubting myself.

From that day on, I brought about a change in my attitude towards life and started on this new journey along with Guru Ji. And this journey was not going to be easy.

***

Since the day I started my spiritual journey, it has been a roller coaster ride. The intensity of my emotions and my physical attributes were at their peak. At first, I did not understand the intensity of the emotions because it was my darker side, which was being manifested in a very intense way. The layers of anger, frustration, low self-esteem, and disbelief started oozing out of my life. Sometimes it will take the form of tears, which keep flowing as if some dirt is being washed out of my life. I would call Guruji and cry for hours over the phone, asking questions about my being. There were so many whys that needed to be answered, and the biggest question was why my relationships with men did not work out and why after every few years, my life would stand at a crucial juncture where I would have to start from scratch, no career, no relationship.

Guruji will make me sit in meditation. Sometimes I would meditate for two to three hours, tears flowing and chanting Om Namah Shivaya would gradually make me feel calm. I kept doing it for months, and slowly and gradually the intensity of the pain in my inner turmoil started subsiding. The focus, which was based on the outer factors, was losing its identity as my focus started shifting to my inner self. I would sometimes get a glimpse of the pure self, which is endowed with all the virtues of happiness, abundance, good health, purity, and freedom. That was a beautiful feeling, and I wanted to stay forever in that realm, but as human beings, we keep falling back. The answer to my whys was still required.

I would meditate every day, and each day was a new experience and a new awakening. The story of my being from birth until now was showing me certain clarity.

Apart from getting certain clarity about me, I became aware of two major phenomena: the presence of the higher self (God's realisation) and the presence of a spiritual guru (complete mentor).

God's Realization

I am a spiritual person, but I never was into the austerity of religion. I always believed in the power of the higher self, which governed everything in the universe, and that's it. Apart from this, I never felt or tried to understand it at any deeper level. I was so engrossed and bound in the chains of karma and my lower self that I never felt like going deep into it.

But the higher self-wanted me to understand it at a deeper level and has been showing me glimpses of his being in very different ways. I will quote an experience: when I was quite young, around 25 years old, after my marriage, my husband took me to a holy shrine in Jammu, which is called Vaishno Devi. I went there just to have fun. I had no devotion or urge to see what was there for me; it was to spend more time with my husband in a different environment. We started our journey to climb the mountains, as it was 14 km going up and down. I am not very fond of climbing, but I continued with it because I had no other choice. Along the way, I noticed many people climbing with great devotion and chanting the name of Durga. For me it was weird. All along the way, my husband kept urging me to chant, but being stubborn, I did not utter a word, and somehow, we reached the shrine and paid our respects to the three pins in the shrine, and that's it. I thought that we had come so far just to see this, and in a minute, we were out of the shrine. I was not at all happy. I rebuked my husband and shouted at him that you had brought me so far just to these stones. The moment I uttered those words, a spark of bright white light blinded my eyes. My entire being was shaken, and automatically I started chanting the name of Durga, unknowingly, till we reached the base of the shrine. That was my first encounter with my higher self, the omnipresent. Again, I was so engrossed in the chaos of my life that I never felt the urge to understand it any further. But my destiny had designed a different path for me, which I was going to uncover after 32 years and that would lead me on this wonderful journey of knowing God at every moment.

Meeting Guruji and rediscovering the higher self- started from day one. There were many questions, many doubts, many fears and many unknown territories that needed to be discovered and explored.

The Guru

God's realization is only possible through a spiritual master, who is the direct descendant of the divine and holds the divine knowledge. Without his grace, our inner selves remain unawaken, we keep indulging in the lower selves, and our spirit remains chained to our body, which is the carrier of our karma. During my journey of spiritual awakening, I realised that we need a guru more than a friend, a son, a husband, or all the wealth of this world. This belief strengthened more during the coming years because a spiritual guru enables us to witness all the riches of the heart and imparts his knowledge for us to walk on the path of God's realization.

It is not easy to encounter a true guru, but how do you realise that he is a true guru? This was my thought when I first met Guruji, as I am not that kind of person who would just believe anyone and become his blind disciple. Because the world is filled with so-called gurus who are working for their personal benefits and making it a profitable business. Although I was drawn to his divine aura when I first met him, this apprehension was there in my mind.

The unique quality of his character made me walk on this path. Firstly, he was not that kind of person who had lakhs of devotees and was sitting on the throne and lecturing on the topics of God. He was very down to earth and would talk and have knowledge of every small to big topic in general life and the world at large. He is simple, straightforward, and loving. He was very gentle with me about the various questions and apprehensions that I was holding in my heart.

As I started knowing him more, I considered myself fortunate to have encountered a true master who was a great and wonderful deity. So many things made me understand that he is not an ordinary being, that I can be blessed by his greatness, and that I can understand the ways of God with him. He never asked for any money or offerings from me; his only concern was to take away my anxieties and sins. Being in his company only or talking to him over the phone would uplift my life, and I will become joyful. This is something not only I have felt but so many other people who know him closely. He has the power to cure the diseases of your body, your soul, and your mind and break the karmic chains of your life.

The guru understands the ways of the world very well and is fully conscious of the law of destiny. He is fully familiar with the ways of God. On one hand, he is a master in spiritual matters, and on the other hand, he is exceedingly humble in his worldly dealings. These characteristics made me drawn to him, seek the knowledge of Param Shiva, and complete my mission in this world.

I, under the protection of such a master, passed through many crises with ease and met many unfavourable circumstances fearlessly. During the

COVID period after my second vaccination, I suffered from acute stomach infections and pain. The pain was so acute, and I felt that my end was near as there was no respite from the medicines. At this moment, Guruji held my hand. He would make me sit in meditation and transfer his energy or power into my body. Slowly and gradually, I started gaining strength and was able to recover after one and a half months. Seeing death so closely, I owe this life to Guru Ji. I know it is my second birth. Writing about him is actually repaying the debt of gratitude.

Apart from healing humans from the pains of their karma, his main concern is to take care of nature. He will equally treat human beings, nature, birds, animals, and water bodies. As I got to know him more closely over the years, I was able to witness his many hidden aspects. He is a person who does not seek the limelight but prefers to work behind the scenes to help humankind. Despite holding so many powers equal to Shiva, he prefers to live as an ordinary human being.

He has immense power, which most of the time leaves me and others speechless. Just by giving you a glance, he will know your past, present, and future. He prefers to stay humble and rarely shows his power.

His concern for humankind is so big that every year he holds a big Havan (Yagya) in Uttarakhand, which is continuously performed by the pandits for days to have good rain and the purification of the mother earth.

Despite being omniscient, he depicts ignorance. He does not attach much importance to miraculous powers; he maintains that, compared to God's miracle of self-manifestation, all others fade into utter insignificance. The entire universe exists in Shiva; is there any greater miracle than this.? Various godly powers reside in him secretly; major sidhis exist in him as a matter of course, and even though he does not display them, they become active in his service automatically of their own accord.

Rain God works at his free will; there have been so many instances when we requested him to make it rain, and it would happen. So many of his disciples are witnesses to this miracle.

In my journey, his only concern is how I can come out of my fears and inhibitions regarding myself and lead the path of God's realization. He never forced any austerities or strict rules for meditation. Moreover, his concern is never to attach a disciple to him; rather, he will keep pushing away from himself and guiding towards himself to get all the solutions to the problems and realise God. Although there is no guided meditation, he keeps a close eye on the progress of the person. He never asks you to renounce any worldly things; according to him, everything is created by God. His only concern is to bring the person out of limited individuality and make the person's inner self shine with meditation.

The guru elevates the disciple, shows them their true nature, and enables them to realize their Shivahood by merging them into Shiva. His power is so potent that it can transform an individual completely. He grants a new life free from sorrow and limits. He makes a person attain perfection amidst worldly life.

The initial phase of my meditation was full of questions regarding my situation. To get the answers, I started interacting with the universe, and to my utter surprise, in return, I was getting answers to all my questions. The first question that I asked was why I have been alone in my journey, not having the support of any male figure in my life, whether my father, my brother, or my two husbands. All the time, I had to pave my way alone under all the circumstances, whether good or bad. The universe responded to this question in such a subtle and loving way that God has always been with me throughout the journey, holding my hand, but I never noticed. This answer not only made me cry but also reflected the fact that yes, he was there. I have fallen down so many times, and each time, a power has encouraged me to get up and move forward. The other question that was bothering me a lot was my failed marriages and my tendency to look for happiness in the outer factors, which would leave me sad and depressed most of the time. I think the answer to this question required lots of inner transformation, so the process started with my daily deep meditation.

I had various experiences in my meditative state related to myself and others, which I will share separately as they were quite unique experiences of the heavenly world. As to my personal life experiences, as inquisitive as I am, I was constantly interacting with the universe, and I was able to witness my three births and try to relate them to my current life, which, to my surprise, held great meaning to my present situation. In all my past lives, I was never married and was in the profession of serving others. My encounter with Guruji was also related to my past life, where it was not completed, and I was bound to meet him in this life to complete a profound mission. As I was connecting some dots, I understood why I always feel intense happiness in serving others and was ready to be there in whatever way I could, whether emotionally, physically, or financially, to provide support. And although I was twice married, I was alone, so the meaning was deep. Still, there was so much to understand, and I kept meditating.

Slowly and gradually, I started feeling happy and joyful and less depressed. The effect of my meditation was showing in my life that my sons sometimes would remark that you are behaving like a kid.

During this period, the first wave of COVID came, and my elder son's marriage got postponed. All the arrangements got cancelled, but despite this, I had faith in God that everything would fall into place, and he would be happily married. He got married on June 1st, 2020, in a

gathering. Later, after eight months of delay, both moved to Australia. And I breathed a sigh of relief.

Now we two were left me and my younger son because of the pandemic, my business was not happening as it required lots of travelling and interaction with people. So again, I was without a career.

Now it had been eight months since I was meditating, so at the initial stage of my confusion, unhappiness was coming to some sort of understanding. Confide in the house; I would just focus on my meditation. As I was going deep into it, I was becoming more aware of the power of self and the grace of the guru, a great master who was transmitting his powers to me to undergo and observe the path of my true nature and feel the bliss of the heavenly realms.

Every day of meditation was a new experience for me. My deep meditation, which would last for hours, was unlocking the mysteries of my being. Sometimes I would witness the lower self that was filled with fear, lack, disappointment, and agony but sometimes I would feel utter joy, happiness, and fearlessness. Both states were mine, and there was a stark difference between them. One was complete, and the other was so incomplete, but both were integral parts of me.

I was aware of the higher self, the pure self, which existed in me and was giving me so much joy, peace and happiness. It was not related to any materialistic thing or attachment to any human relationship. I wanted to stay in that state of pure bliss.

But……….

Why can't I stay in this state forever?

Why do I fail to see the truth?

Why do I suffer?

Why do I live my life with a limited self?

And there were many more unanswered questions. But now these questions were just not related to my situation, where I felt like a victim of the circumstances, but these were more deep questions that required answers to further strengthen my awakening.

Guruji would very strictly yet compassionately encourage me to go deep within to look for these answers, as this was my journey and I needed to unlock its mysteries. Sometimes I felt that Guruji threw me into the deep water and wanted me to swim my way up. I would be frustrated as it was a unique journey for me, but I was very sure I would not get any help from him. But I was determined to unlock the mysteries of life.

Meanwhile, in my personal life, things were moving at a fast pace. My son's marriage, which was postponed due to COVID, happened after three months in the month of June 2020. Although there were many hurdles, because of my staunch faith in Guruji and in my meditation, things went smoothly, even to my amazement, and both my son and daughter-in-law moved back to Australia.

But during this period, a very strange thing happened. All my relatives suddenly stopped talking to me as they were holding me responsible for not inviting them to the wedding of my son, which was held during COVID time, a situation that was not in my control.

Initially, I felt bad because I was abandoned by everyone, but as I grew in my meditation, I understood that it was the design of the universe that was forcing me to be alone on this journey. After a few months I accepted the situation, and moreover, I was also not in the mental state to talk to anyone as lots of things were happening in my inner world, my physical attributes were also changing, and my sleep pattern was all shaken up. And at this next level of my meditation, I was not understanding all these happenings. But I was constantly in touch with Guruji, as my desire to explore more was growing day by day.

This was a new realm that I was discovering. As the days became more devoted to the Guruji and to my meditation, more and more marvelous experiences occurred in my life. But sometimes, due to the impurities of the heart and mind or falling again into the realm of human beings who have lots of attachments and desires, I would fall back to the same. But I was not ready to give up.

My body was undergoing many changes; the changes started from my tip of the toe to the top of my head. Various aches and pains started occurring in my body, which would last for days. Sometimes I was sleeping for 20 hours and sometimes only two hours. My eating routine was changed; sometimes I wouldn't have the desire to eat anything; sometimes I would just have very little food, but my energy levels were always high, so I wouldn't have the desire for anything. When I asked Guruji about all these happenings, he said that the Kundalini Shakti, aroused by the Guru's grace, would have such impacts. It penetrates the system of 72,000 nerves, purifies and strengthens all the circuits that carry blood and prana, then releases vital energy into them, thus transforming the body. And all the happenings in your environment are also part of your awakening. You should remain unaffected by all these transformations because your life is being redesigned from the inside to the outside. In this state, I left my friend's circle as well. The outer world started decreasing as I was becoming more introverted, and to my utter surprise, I was enjoying this phase. I was just managing the household and providing food for my son on a timely basis. And the rest of the time I was in slumber.

All my senses started to awaken. I understood that my thoughts, worries, and desires were having a direct effect on my body. My awakening was introducing me to a new self where I was releasing all the traumas of my past, which I had accumulated not from this lifetime but from the past many lives. Coming face-to-face with this reality was very disturbing. I never knew that these feelings were directly affecting my health. More aches and pains mean I am still holding grudges and painful emotions that are coming out in the form of diabetes and hypertension. I was suffering from trigeminal neuralgia, which is an incurable disease, and was on a heavy dose of antidepressants for the past five years.

I would be drowned in the sea of suffering. All the past traumas would hit me so hard on the face, which would lead to emotional drains. Sometimes I would get so scared that I felt that there was something majorly wrong with me. Maybe I was suffering from some incurable illness, and I would run to the doctor and get all my tests done, and to my utter surprise, all the tests would come back normal. As for my mental status, I would feel that I would go mad as so many past emotions were affecting my state of mind. This was a dark period of my life.

Talking to Guruji would make me feel better. He was very calm during this time, as I would call him in great panic because this is my last day on this earth. I am not going to survive. He would gently laugh and tell me all the dirt is being removed from your body and mind; don't worry, nothing is going to happen to you, and he would encourage me to sit in meditation.

After the waves of physical and mental emotions would subside, I would again be drowned in immense bliss. My body would become so light that all the pains and negative and dark emotions would disappear. It is very difficult to explain the feeling of bliss in words. Time and again, I was being introduced to my real self, which has no worries, fear, lack, or sickness. It was part of me, the real me, which is buried in a five-foot body. The lightness of my body will make me feel like feathering the bliss, the peace, the calmness of my mind. I can stay there forever. The feeling is intoxicated; the more I was away from the outer world, the more I was coming closer to my inner self. As if the universe, the higher self, wanted me to stay in this realm. So many questions were there to be answered again.

What is my true self?

What is my true destination? Is this body, or my existence, my destination?

The desire to know the answer to all these questions would make me sit again in deep meditation which would take me to my origin. I am not just the seed of my mother and father's sperm; I am more than that. I am just not a name, the body, my surroundings, or my family. I am more than this, which makes me complete. What is that?

In our conscious minds, we all know that we were created by God; in fact, the entire universe was created by him. But apart from this, we don't understand, or we are so caught up in our daily lives or by the fact that our ego self refuses to let us see outside the box, and we remain in this reality and lead our existence, bound by our karma as a smaller ME.

But our creator is perfect; he is absolute; he has no lack, no fear, no apprehensions, no grudges; for ages he has been bestowing his love on us without holding.

When we see the universe, we see no lack, and similarly, he has created humans with the same energy, which means that if our source is absolute and perfect, so are we. A caged bird cannot understand the freedom of flight or the joy of being free from all kinds of limitations. Similarly, we human beings are so into our existence that we cannot even imagine what we are.

The effects of my meditation gradually started reflecting in every area of my body. I was able to cure my depression and left my anti-depressant medicine totally. My diabetes and hypertension were also under control. I lost 13 kg of weight, and my face had a different kind of glow, which was making me look years younger.

The other aspect that I came to understand during this process was that human beings have the capability to heal themselves, whether it is emotional illness or physical illness. This is also a gift of the higher power, which resides in us silently to ignite it. We stopped listening to the outer world.

The World of Higher Consciousness

Things were happening for me at different levels. I would regularly get up at 3 a.m. and sit for my meditation; there were no set parameters. I would just sit quietly with closed eyes and chant OM Namah Shivaya. The sound of the voice would uplift me so much that sometimes I would sit like that for 2-3 hours, which would leave me deeply satisfied and happy. During these days of my meditation, unique experiences started occurring. While sitting in my meditation, I slipped into a tandra state, which is a state where you are neither sleeping nor dreaming. In this state, I would see prophetic sights that would give me immense surprises. I would feel that I have been meditating for years. This is not my first time meditating like this, and I am very fortunate person that I have been chosen by Guruji to walk through this. He is omnipresent, aware of every happening, yet conducts himself in a very humble way with no ego or arrogance. Although he is Vishnu, Shiva, Brahma, and Kapil Muni, The entire universe bows down to his powers. Vishnu ji gets up from his sheshnag to offer him honour and offers his seat. All the Devas, Rishi Muni, hold meetings with him to discuss the workings of the Brahmand (the universe).

I consider myself very fortunate to witness all these gatherings and scary events.

I have never visited the Padmanabha Temple nor was I aware of its history, as I was never much into temples. But to my utter surprise, in my meditation, I was able to see everything in that temple, from the statue of Vishnu sitting on Sheshnag to the locked doors that was locked for many years. The sixth door I saw opened. My curiosity drove me to search on the internet for information about this temple and its history. I was in shock that it was the same as what I saw in my meditation.

These mystic things didn't stop here; every day in my meditation, I was witnessing new things. There were times when my entire body would be engrossed in white light. The light used to be so bright as if thousands of suns had emerged, but light will not burn your eyes but would have a calm and soothing effect on my nerves. My room used to be filled with the smell of roses or incense, which would appear from nowhere. Sometimes my son would say, "Mom, your room smells so nice." I was in bewilderment, but I was so happy and joyful.

My room has become my beautiful abode every night. I was looking forward to new experiences. In the state of Tandra, I visited many other Loks. Those worlds were entirely different from this one. There were so many saints in pure white clothes performing yagas. Very beautiful and gentle-looking males and females were roaming there. They were so youthful and free of disease; a gentle breeze would be flowing in that land; all were so happy and content, as if you were in heaven.

There was a day when I witnessed a very different world. It was full of garbage, and a foul smell was coming out of there. I wanted to run away from that place, but my consciousness kept going deep into it. I saw men and women there naked, sitting on the heap of filth, dejected and quite scary and ugly. They seemed to be in a lot of pain. There was not much to eat or drink. This incident shook me. I stumbled out of this meditation quite sad and upset. The next day, first thing in the morning, I called Guruji and told him about this spiritual experience.

He gently laughed and told me that you are witnessing both the world, heaven, and hell. Don't worry it all exists. You are fortunate that you are able to see it with your eyes, so you can differentiate and focus more on doing good to yourself and others. For a few days I just kept contemplating these two experiences. I started feeling a change in my inner being. At first, I felt a disconnect from the world; for me, nothing held any meaning. This made me think deeply about why we run after materialistic things, worldly pleasures, jealousy, anger, and competition. Nothing holds meaning after we die. Only our good deeds are going to be our allies.

For a few days I was in this mode, then again, the nudge to be up at 3:00 am made me sit in meditation. This wake-up call at 3 a.m. has been part of my life's journey for the past 20 years. At first, I was not aware of the meaning of this call, but after walking on the path of my spiritual awakening, I understood that this was not just a wake-up call. The universe is trying to connect with me at that time so I can write a different story about my life.

During this period of my meditation, I drifted to other worlds. Still, writing about these experiences gives me goosebumps. One day a very beautiful white horse came to me; the whiteness and aura of that horse were not from this world; it was a horse from Devlok. Very happily and joyfully, he took me to Mount Kailash, the divine place endowed with such a beauty that is indescribable. The scent of the place and the flowers that were growing there held a different kind of feeling. I got immersed in the beauty of the place and sat there for hours, immersed in the divine beauty and bliss.

And the other day I saw a big city where the palace was made of gold and silver. The men and women were wearing white robes, and their height was around 20 feet. They were such divine figures, free from sorrow and disease and shining with glorious light. All the paths were bedded with beautiful flowers, trees laden with fruits, and various kinds of birds, and the breeze was filled with celestial perfume. The entire place was holding the delight of celestial feeling, and then I saw an elephant so huge in white that it was the elephant of God Indra. (I would like to remind my readers that I was seeing all these sights in Tandra Lok while sitting in my meditation.)

I opened my eyes and closed them again to behold the beautiful sight lingering before my inner eyes. As I recollected these visions, I was stuck with wonder, and I wanted to perceive every detail in my inner consciousness, so I kept writing down every detail of my beautiful journeys to heaven, hell, Mount Kailash, and Inderlok. All these experiences made me realise the scriptures that were written by our sages, where they mentioned that these worlds were valid and existed. Those scriptures were true; they must have composed them after obtaining omniscience through meditation. We human beings don't understand and acknowledge these things, as our human eyes have not witnessed such worlds, but being on this path, I, as a person, felt so blessed and fortunate that I have been chosen to walk this path.

Naad

After two years of meditation, I developed a sound in my right ear. It began with thumping and gradually moved towards the sound of a whistle or the sound of cricket whispering in the night. I got alarmed and visited many ENT specialists for the cure, as they were suggesting that it could be tinnitus, which is affecting my right ear and slowly can affect my hearing as well. As I am in habit of sharing things with Guruji, I told him about this current happening. As always, unalarmed he said you are not suffering from any disease, as these are the voices of the universe. This is Anhad. Naad, I was shocked why I would be listening to such noises, but I didn't know it was part of my spiritual awakening. In fear, I kept taking the treatment from the doctor; the medication and the test did not help me subside these noises, and ultimately, I gave up on all the treatment and surrendered to the universe and attentively started listening to the voices. There were many different voices coming from my right ear. Sometimes they would become so subtle that I would enjoy them and be lost in the world of music, which was giving me pleasure and peace. I would float on the waves of this new musical ecstasy, but at times I could not sleep. Usually, lack of sleep affects the mind adversely, but nothing of this kind happened to me. In spite of the loss of sleep, I remained active and joyful. I did not seem to need sleep. However, I was eating much less and also looked somewhat slim. Gradually, I was hearing nothing for longer durations, even while doing my daily routines. In fact, I hear it all the time—eating, sleeping, coming going—and it will become louder or quieter depending on my various emotions. While experiencing such mystical happenings I was continuing my journey.

Mysticism of Guruji

As I have mentioned the mystical aspects of Guruji in my writing, I want to elaborate more on this topic, as this uniqueness was not only felt by me but by many others who have encounter him. Being an empath, whenever I see someone suffering from their deep karmic situations, I instantly introduce them to Guruji, be it my friends or anyone in my known circle. Every person who has been in contact with him has been able to feel the grace and aura of his mystical being. Not only have they been able to come out of their sufferings, but they have been able to transform their situation dramatically, be it financial, relational, health, or many other worldly matters. The desire to live a normal married life was always very close to my heart, seeing him do miracles with the lives of others and mine. I would ask him to change my situation so I could also live a happy life. Although I was not in talks with my husband, the desire to be with him and spend the rest of the years, especially the later years, as I was very scared to spend the final years alone, was so deep that sometimes I would literally beg or fight with Guruji to sort this situation out. But to my utter surprise, neither he would listen to me, nor would he make any effort in this area. As always, very calmly and gently, he would encourage me to live a happy and peaceful life. But a mysterious look in his eyes would leave me in a dilemma.

Writing about him is like showing the light to the sun. I consider myself to be very fortunate, as I have been chosen to write about him. This seems to be the ultimate purpose as this will be recorded for years to come.

Turn of Events

My personal life was about to take a different turn. I was unaware of it.

My husband had again stopped coming to my house but was in touch with my sons, as both my sons would feel a deep sense of gratitude towards him for raising them, and I was ready to go to any length to support him. So, to support him, my elder son was sending him money on a monthly basis and supporting him a huge amount whenever he asked to expand his business. For all of us, there was a hope that once he settled his business and took care of his mother, he would come back, and it was our duty to support him unconditionally.

After two years of my elder son's marriage, I started looking for a match for my younger son, as I wanted to complete my responsibility. He met a girl on the dating app, and they were in talks to further explore their chances for matchmaking. In the meantime, the girl's father, without my knowledge, searched about my husband's and my background as things might end up in marriage.

To my utter surprise and shock, the girl's family came to us with very earth-shattering news. They told us that my husband is not living in Bareilly, a town in Uttar Pradesh, where supposedly he is setting up his business and living with his mother; instead, he is in Delhi only, married six years ago, and has a daughter. This was a blow to all three of us. After confronting him, he accepted that it was all true. My hope died. Now I understood the mysterious look in Guruji's eye and his continuous encouragement for me to focus on myself and be happy. As things were unfolding, I came to know that he had minted lakhs of rupees from my elder son and was hoping to continually do that. After that day, all three of us broke our ties with him. It was a big emotional setback for all of us.

This may sound odd, but my last hope died after all the happenings. I was still hopeful that someday he would return and we could live a happy life. I wanted to move to another country or another state to start over, leaving behind all the heartache. To do this, I started encouraging my younger son to look for some opportunity so we could move out. He kept trying, as after the COVID, nothing seemed to be working out. My desperation was increasing day by day. I was constantly in touch with Guruji, as I was again shattered and emotionally vulnerable. His calm self was again encouraging me to trust the process and stay happy. Although it was very difficult, I tried to come to terms with the situation.

After six months, my prayer was answered, and my younger son was offered a transfer through his company to Riyadh, Saudi Arabia. As it was a good opportunity, and we were looking for change, he accepted it, and we moved to Riyadh at the beginning of the year 2022.

It was again a new journey for me, and I was looking forward to it. I was feeling as if I was shedding the old self and moving towards the new self. Despite the apprehensions of a totally different country, I was looking forward to it.

The initial months took us a while to settle down, as it was a totally new country with a language barrier and different cultural background. My son will go to the office, and I would stay back at home, managing the general household things and doing some cooking. As in any country abroad, everything was done by yourself; house help was not available. This was also a big change for me because back home I was so used to having help. After coping with this initial change, I settled down to the daily routine.

The Silence

I was unaware that I would be tested at different levels. I was surrounded by silence. The silence of my surroundings was showing me a different me.

Being alone at home made me realise that silence has its own noise; these are not the noises of the outer world but the noise of your mind. All the time I was indulged in self-talk that was not very productive. My past life was coming back to me in loads; all the events and happenings became fresh in my mind, and the initial joy of moving to a different set of environments started dying down. No, I would think this is some other phase that I have to pass through. I will be okay.

I was encouraging myself every day. The noises started emerging and became very loud, to the extent that I started fearing them. I would feel that I would go crazy as I was standing face-to-face with myself. The stark realities of my inner self were emerging.

This time they were very different from back home. I used to have such thoughts, but they would be dissolved in the daily routine. The old wounds, my emotional instability, and my insecurity started haunting my days. According to Guruji, this was the best period of life. He would encourage me to stay calm, he would say to fulfil your duties towards your family, and he would devote more time to meditation.

Slowly, I started enjoying my solitude, as it was different from loneliness. The more I was getting away from the outer world, the closer I was coming to myself. The real ME, which was buried under the debris of so many illusions, slowly started emerging. It was as if I were peeling the layers of an onion to bring out the real me.

Oh, is it that easy? The older ME was not ready to let go. Since I met Guruji and started my spiritual journey, nothing has been going according to my plans. Although things were happening for the best, they seemed to be out of my control. The years of thinking, planning, and executing seemed to be drifting away from me. The more I was trying to control the things, the more they were slipping from my hand.

This was making me uneasy. My previous self-refused—the older ME kept coming back. I was again in desperate talks with Guruji, and he said to let go and surrender. Surrender to what was my next question, to which he again nudged me to find the answer by myself. I would sit in long hours of meditation to find the answer I was assured by the universe and encouraged to trust the process and be calm.

One day I completely surrendered to the law, to the universe, and to the Guruji and felt like a baby whose needs are taken care of by the parents, or like a child in the womb who is not worried by any outcome and sits peacefully in the womb.

The feeling was very soothing and starkly different from the feeling of taking control of things and planning and executing the future. I am in total bliss. The bliss of knowing a power is guiding me, holding my hand, nurturing me, and taking me forward to my purpose.

During all these significant changes in being, one thing was becoming more and more clear, and a sound was coming very clearly in my mind: I have not signed off yet.

There is more in me that I should share with the world. This book is the answer to purpose.

www.ingramcontent.com/pod-product-compliance
Lightning Source LLC
LaVergne TN
LVHW061631070526
838199LV00071B/6642